BASED ON THE PUBLIC TELEVISION SERIES

BASEBALL
THE · AMERICAN · EPIC

25
GREAT MOMENTS

BY GEOFFREY C. WARD
AND KEN BURNS, WITH S. A. KRAMER

ILLUSTRATED WITH PHOTOGRAPHS

ALFRED A. KNOPF ❦ NEW YORK

CONTENTS

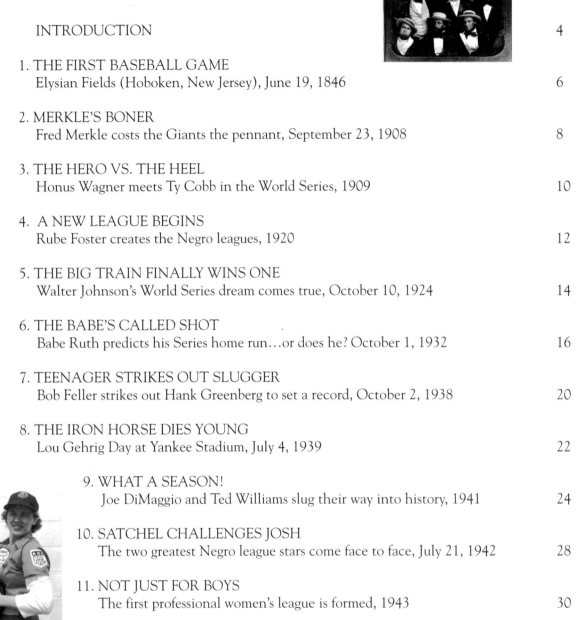

INTRODUCTION

BASEBALL AND AMERICA have grown up together. The history of the game is almost as long as the history of the nation. In fact, the two are so connected that what's happened to one has usually happened to the other. Both have been changed by war, by economic hardship, and by the struggle for racial equality. When baseball experiences its greatest moments, the whole nation watches, sharing in the drama and excitement.

This is a book about some of those moments—Jackie Robinson becoming the first African American in the majors, Nolan Ryan pitching an unheard-of seventh no-hitter, Hank Aaron shattering a home run mark that had stood for 39 years. You'll read about players like Joe DiMaggio, who were champions every day, and others, like Don Larsen, who were terrific only once. You'll relive brief moments of glory and hours of suspense.

Of course, fans will always argue about which moments are baseball's best. This book will tell you about some that can't be overlooked. From the first real game in 1846 through the homer that won the 1993 World Series, here are 25 of the most exciting moments in the history of our national pastime.

THE FIRST BASEBALL GAME

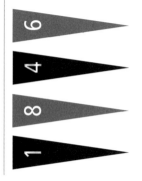

1846

JUNE 19, 1846. The Elysian Fields in Hoboken, New Jersey. Two New York teams arrived by ferry to try a new way of playing a game called "base ball." No Manhattan field was big enough, so they rented a spot across the Hudson River for $75 a year.

The teams were the New York Knickerbockers and the New York Base Ball Club. Not a single player was paid to take the field. They were all from the wealthier parts of society—stockbrokers and salesmen, a photographer and a marshal. They didn't have mitts or uniforms.

The game played that day was the first true version of modern baseball. Before, Americans had played ball-and-stick games like rounders and cricket, British sports that had been popular on these shores since the 1700s. But Alexander Cartwright and other Knickerbockers had devised a new set of rules. In cricket the ball was always fair, but in baseball there would be foul lines. Rounders allowed runners to be hit with the ball for an out, but in baseball the runner would have to be tagged or thrown out. These new rules made baseball faster and more exciting than the British games it was based on.

The New York Base Ball Club walloped the Knickerbockers that day, 23–1. Far from annoyed, the Knickerbockers enjoyed themselves. Afterward, they drank champagne and ate a good supper.

THE NEW YORK KNICKERBOCKERS

The new game was a big success. Within 10 years, there were 50 clubs in New York City alone. People from all walks of life—doctors, bakers, shipbuilders—organized their own teams. Pioneers then took the sport west, and Civil War soldiers carried it across the nation.

In 1905, Chicago White Sox owner Albert Spalding helped spread the story that Civil War hero Abner Doubleday had invented baseball in Cooperstown, New York, in 1839. But in truth, the game we play today evolved directly from the Knickerbockers' set of rules.

Baseball is now played throughout the world and watched by millions of fans each year. Little did the Knickerbockers know that their friendly game would become America's national pastime.

"AT SUCH TIMES WE WERE BOYS AGAIN."

—FRANK PIDGEON, OF BROOKLYN'S ECKFORD BASE BALL CLUB

AN ENGRAVING OF AN
EARLY BASEBALL MATCH
AT THE ELYSIAN FIELDS

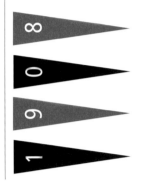

SEPTEMBER 23, 1908. New York City. The Chicago Cubs were facing the New York Giants with the pennant at stake. Every game was a must-win situation. In the bottom of the ninth, the score was tied at 1–1, and the Giants had runners on first and third. But there were two outs.

Fred Merkle was the runner on first.

The next man up lined a single. The run came home from third. It looked like a Giants' victory, and cheering fans swarmed the field.

But Johnny Evers, the Cubs' second baseman, noticed that Merkle never reached second base. Merkle, a 19-year-old rookie, was frightened by the crowd. Convinced that the game was over, he raced off the field. But he had forgotten an important rule of baseball: the Cubs could get a force-out if he didn't touch second. If the ball beat Fred to the base, there would be three outs, and the Giants' run wouldn't count.

Fred disappeared—but so did the ball. No one could find it on a field jammed with people. Finally, a Giants' coach spotted it and hurled it into the stands. A fan in a brown hat grabbed it and headed for the exit.

Two Cubs chased him, knocked him down, and threw the ball to Evers, who jumped on the base. Merkle was ruled out, and the game was declared a tie because the fans could not be removed from the field. The two teams later ended the season dead even, and a playoff game had to be scheduled. The pennant would go to the winner.

In the playoff game, the Cubs sent Mordecai "Three Finger" Brown to the mound. Brown was missing his index finger, and his pinky was paralyzed. But many believed his injury only made his curve more wicked. Brown had to face the Giants' Christy Mathewson, who had won 37 games that year. But Brown outpitched the great Christy, sending the Cubs to the World Series—and sending the Giants home.

New York fans refused to forgive Merkle. He played for another 14 years, finishing his career with a respectable .273 average. But he could never escape from the shadow of one of the biggest blunders in baseball history. His mistake will forever be known, simply, as "Merkle's Boner."

FRED MERKLE

"I KNEW MERKLE
     MIGHT MAKE A
BONEHEAD"
—JOHNNY EVERS

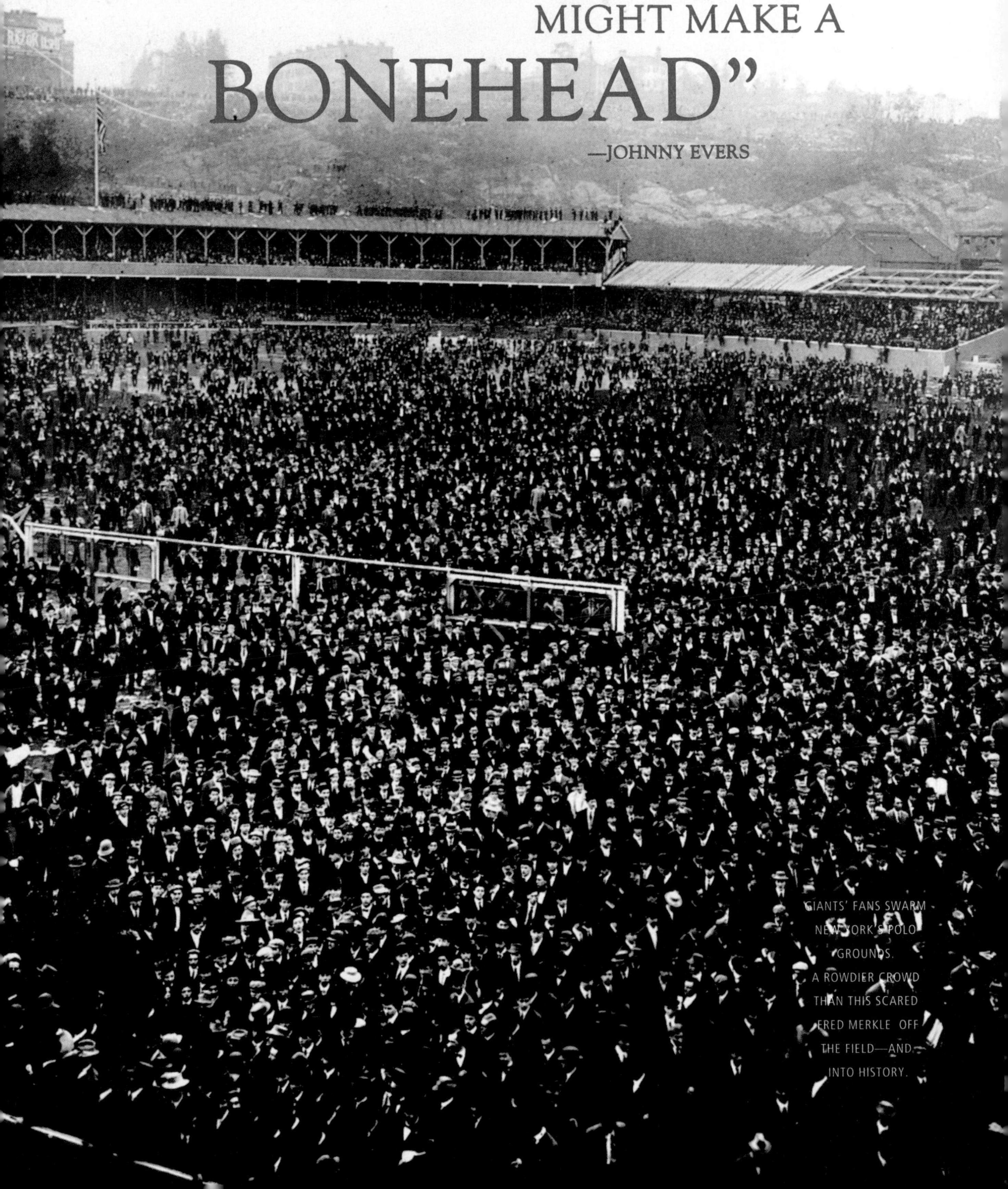

GIANTS' FANS SWARM
NEW YORK'S POLO
GROUNDS.
A ROWDIER CROWD
THAN THIS SCARED
FRED MERKLE OFF
THE FIELD—AND
INTO HISTORY.

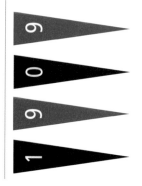

THIS HONUS WAGNER CARD WAS MADE BY A CIGARETTE COMPANY. HONUS DIDN'T SMOKE, AND WHEN HE OBJECTED, THE CARD WAS DISCONTINUED. THE CARDS ARE NOW WORTH ABOUT $450,000 EACH.

THE OPENING GAME of the 1909 World Series. It was the Detroit Tigers vs. the Pittsburgh Pirates. Many believed, however, that it was really Ty Cobb ("the Georgia Peach") against Honus Wagner ("the Flying Dutchman"). They were the game's greatest stars, but they had never faced each other before. Their different personalities were well known—but who was the better player?

Cobb constantly picked fights—not only with his opponents but with teammates and fans as well. Most players despised him, and many thought he was truly insane. But he was a sensational hitter, at one time winning nine batting titles in a row.

Wagner, on the other hand, was one of the most popular men in the game. Modest and kind, he enjoyed poking fun at himself. He was bow-legged and looked clumsy, but he flew around the bases. In the field he caught everything, and at the plate he smashed the ball.

Before the game, the two stars shook hands. But when the action began, they stopped being friendly. Cobb planned to steal a base quickly to prove no one could stop him. Wagner was baseball's greatest shortstop, but Cobb thought he could scare him. Legend has it that when Cobb reached first, he called out to Wagner: "Watch out, Krauthead…I'll cut you to pieces!"

The insult didn't work. "Come ahead," Wagner said. Accepting the dare, Cobb charged second and slid right at Wagner with his spikes up.

"I'LL CUT YOU TO PIECES!"

—TY COBB

Wagner wasn't surprised. Ty often played dirty—he'd do anything to win. To avoid getting spiked, many fielders would often step aside and just give him the base. But Wagner didn't back off. He tagged Cobb hard in the mouth. Later, Wagner claimed that it took three stitches to close Cobb's split lip.

Honus Wagner's Pirates won the series. Wagner outhit Cobb, and even stole more bases. Still, no one can say for sure who was a better player. Wagner holds the National League record for most batting championships (eight) and RBI titles (four). But Cobb has the highest lifetime batting average (.367). He is second in total hits (4,191) and first in runs scored (2,246).

Fans may argue forever about which player was better. But at least, for one World Series, baseball fans got to watch the game's two greatest stars—one loved, the other hated—play head-to-head.

TY COBB PLOWS INTO THIRD, KNOCKING THE THIRD BASEMAN INTO THE AIR. MANY OPPOSING FIELDERS WOULD GET OUT OF THE WAY AND GIVE THE HARD-CHARGING COBB THE BASE.

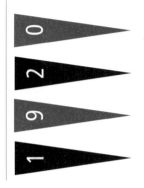

1883. Moses Fleetwood Walker entered the major leagues. He was a talented catcher, but he was spurned immediately by his teammates. Fleet hadn't done anything wrong—he just wasn't the right color. One pitcher simply ignored his signals, saying he wouldn't take orders from a black man.

Back then, many Americans felt that whites and blacks should be on separate teams. White players forced major league owners to ban blacks from their clubs. The majors stayed whites-only until 1947.

But nothing stopped African-American men from playing baseball. They formed their own teams, which featured some of America's greatest athletes. One of them was a superb pitcher named Andrew "Rube" Foster. Foster knew the game well, and had a talent for developing players and for making money. In partnership with a white man, he bought and managed his own club.

Black baseball was exciting. Foster and the other managers stressed speed and daring on the base paths, and the hit-and-run play. Large crowds turned out to watch them. But they had no league to schedule games or manage finances, and white owners kept trying to take over the sport.

So in 1920, Foster called a meeting of black team owners. He had an exciting idea—a whole new league just for blacks. The league not only would organize the teams and control their games, but would also show fans that blacks played as well as whites. Foster also hoped the majors would someday welcome all races. When that day came, the athletes in his league would, he said, be "ready…for integration."

Eight teams combined to form the Negro National League. Rube was appointed to run it. On May 2, 1920, the first game was played in Indianapolis. The Indianapolis ABCs defeated the Chicago Giants, 4–2.

Many black fans turned out to support their teams. The league was so successful that a group of white businessmen formed the rival Eastern Colored League. But when the Great Depression caused millions of

RUBE FOSTER

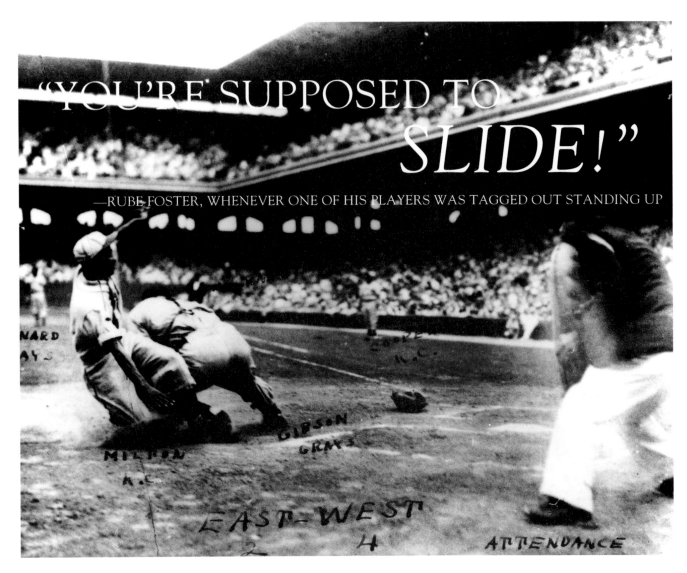

"YOU'RE SUPPOSED TO *SLIDE!*"

—RUBE FOSTER, WHENEVER ONE OF HIS PLAYERS WAS TAGGED OUT STANDING UP

Americans to lose their jobs, it proved hard to keep the leagues going. By 1931, both leagues had disbanded.

Black teams continued to play baseball, inspiring young African Americans throughout the country, and new Negro leagues were formed. While many brilliant black players were cheated of major league careers, these leagues kept the dream of professional baseball alive for blacks. Then, in 1947, Jackie Robinson became the first black man in over fifty years to play in the majors. At last the sport called America's game could be played by *all* men.

THE BIG TRAIN FINALLY WINS ONE

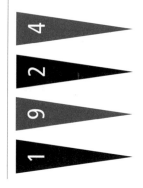

WASHINGTON, D.C. The seventh game of the 1924 World Series. The score was 3–3 in the top of the ninth. One of history's worst teams, the Washington Senators, was battling the New York Giants. The Senators had never played in a championship before.

They needed a reliever, so Walter Johnson took the mound. Unlike pitchers of today, Johnson both started and relieved. He was the greatest right-hander ever, as well as baseball's nicest pitcher. If he was ahead in a game, he'd let rookies get hits. He never threw at batters—if he accidentally hit one, he helped him up. He got his nickname—"the Big Train"—because his fastball seemed as powerful as a locomotive.

But Johnson was tired today. He was 36—old for a ballplayer. He'd already lost two games in the Series. Now he was in trouble with just one out in the inning. Johnson had always been on losing teams—this was his last shot at a title. Somehow he gathered his strength and struck out the next two batters.

But the Senators couldn't rally. Three innings went by. Johnson was exhausted. Still, he struck hitters out. There were men on base every inning, yet he didn't let them score.

With the score still tied in the bottom of the 12th, the Senators managed to put a man on second. There were already two out when the batter grounded to third. It looked like an easy play until the ball hit a pebble and bounced over the fielder's head—and the runner scored!

Tears filled Johnson's eyes. The Senators had won the game—and the Series. Johnson, determined to win just once, had led the way to victory. First in shutouts (110) and second in victories (416), Walter Johnson left his mark on the record books. On this day, he won the game and—almost single-handedly—gave the Senators their only world championship.

WALTER JOHNSON

"THE GOOD LORD COULDN'T BEAR TO SEE WALTER JOHNSON LOSE AGAIN."

—JACK BENTLEY, LOSING PITCHER

MUDDY RUEL RUNS HOME TO SCORE THE WINNING RUN IN THE BOTTOM OF THE 12TH INNING, GIVING WALTER JOHNSON AND THE SENATORS THEIR ONLY CHAMPIONSHIP.

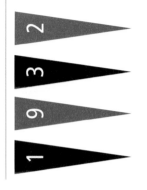

1 9 3 2

WRIGLEY FIELD, CHICAGO. October 1, 1932. The New York Yankees faced the Cubs. It was the fifth inning of the third game of the World Series. Suddenly the Cubs' fans started to boo. The Yankees' number-three hitter, the most famous athlete in the world, had stepped into the on-deck circle. George Herman "Babe" Ruth, baseball's first and greatest slugger, stood there with his big, heavy bat.

Until the Babe came along, baseball had no real home run hitter. He began his career in the "dead ball" era, when 10 homers could lead the league. He started out as a pitcher for the Boston Red Sox, but he was sure that if he played every game, he would be able to clout homer after homer. Hardly anyone believed him—until 1919. That year, when the Babe wasn't pitching, he played the outfield and blasted a total of 29 home runs. Fans were amazed—the rest of his team hit just four.

In 1920, the Babe became a full-time outfielder for the Yankees and slammed an astonishing 54 home runs. That was more than the total hit by any other American League team. Crowds began to follow him wherever he went. Attendance tripled for every game he played. All of America wanted to see the Babe smack one.

Before the Babe, baseball's biggest stars were men who could get that clutch hit whenever their team needed one. But Ruth single-handedly changed the game, making it a sport for sluggers. In 1927, he smashed 60 home runs. It was a record no one thought would ever be broken.

YANKEE STADIUM—"THE HOUSE THAT RUTH BUILT"

But now "the Bambino" was 37, and overweight. Many fans felt he was past his prime. The Babe, though, still believed in himself.

The score was tied as he stepped into the batter's box. Some players on the Cubs' bench shouted insults at him. When the first pitch was a strike, there were cries of "Baboon!" and "Potbelly!" Always the show-man, the Babe smiled and raised one finger. One strike, he was saying, was no problem.

The umpire called the next two pitches balls. The next crossed the

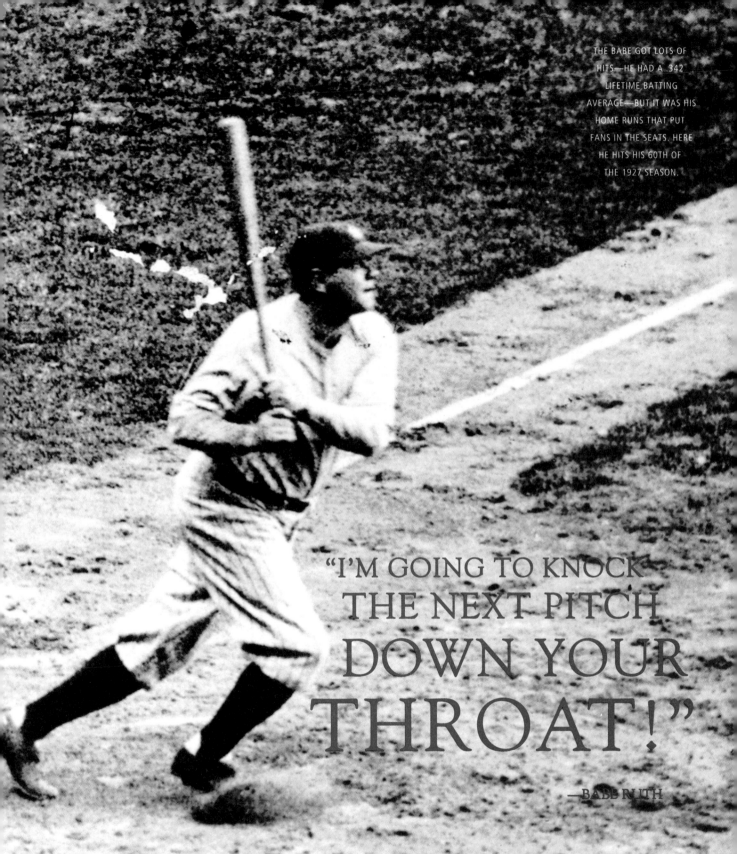

THE BABE GOT LOTS OF
HITS—HE HAD A .342
LIFETIME BATTING
AVERAGE—BUT IT WAS HIS
HOME RUNS THAT PUT
FANS IN THE SEATS. HERE
HE HITS HIS 60TH OF
THE 1927 SEASON.

"I'M GOING TO KNOCK
THE NEXT PITCH
DOWN YOUR
THROAT!"

—BABE RUTH

plate—strike two. The crowd hooted and hollered. A Cub yelled out: "You're just a tramp."

The Babe calmly rubbed dirt on his hands, then looked at the Cubs' dugout and raised two fingers. Now there was just one strike to go. "Only takes one to hit it," he said aloud. Some people thought he then pointed to the center field bleachers.

The Babe waited at the plate. At last the pitcher delivered. It was a change-up, low and away, but that didn't bother the Babe. He could whack homers off balls just above his shoe tops.

The Babe stepped into the pitch, swinging the bat smoothly. The ball shot at the sky and kept going—right into the center field bleachers!

It was the longest home run hit in Wrigley Field up to that time. The fans couldn't believe it. In disgust, they threw garbage on the field. Laughing, Ruth circled the bases, saying to himself, "You lucky bum, you lucky bum." When he rounded third, he clasped his hands over his head.

The Yanks won the game, and then the Series. The Babe's at-bat became one of the most famous ever. To this day people still argue about whether he really called his shot. Could he actually have pointed to the spot where he hit the ball? A home movie of the game shows the Babe pointing, but it's unclear exactly where.

No matter what's decided, the Babe's legend will live on. He drank too much, ate too much, and had trouble obeying rules. But he was also generous and warm—the kind of man who would visit a poor, sick child in a hospital. When he left, there'd be a hundred-dollar bill somewhere on the bed.

BABE RUTH

On the field he was just as dramatic. He hit homers more often than anyone else (every 11.76 times at bat) and has the highest slugging average ever (.690). He was baseball's greatest clutch hitter, driving in a run every 3.79 times at bat. He ranks second in runs scored (2,174), home runs (714), and RBIs (2,211).

Babe Ruth gave baseball some of its most exciting moments. But of all his tremendous feats, the Called Shot stands out. Today, no player would dare do what the Babe did. He was brash and bold—but he was also the best. That is why the story of the Babe's Called Shot remains one of baseball's most beloved legends.

THIS STILL FROM A
FAN'S HOME MOVIE
SHOWS THE BABE
CALLING HIS SHOT
—OR DOES IT?

THE BAMBINO
SURROUNDED BY
SOME OF HIS
MANY FANS

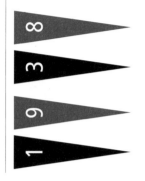

1938

OCTOBER 2, 1938. America was in the midst of the Great Depression, and the threat of war hung over the world. But on this last day of the season, sports fans were thinking about something else. In Cleveland, the Indians were playing the Detroit Tigers, and fans came to see if the Tigers' Hank Greenberg could make baseball history.

Greenberg was one of the best power hitters ever. A two-time MVP, Hank had knocked in 183 runs the previous year—one shy of Lou Gehrig's American League record. And this year, Greenberg was chasing a legend. He had 58 home runs—two short of Babe Ruth's season record. Today was his last chance to tie or break it.

Greenberg was baseball's first Jewish star. Because of his religion, some players and fans insulted him. Hank ignored them—he let his bat do his arguing. Unlike some earlier Jewish athletes, this future Hall-of-Famer refused to change his name. Jewish fans across America responded by treating him like a hero.

Now Hank had to face Bob Feller, the Indians' teenage sensation. Only 19, Feller already had one of the greatest fastballs ever. The radar gun didn't exist yet, so no one knew how swift his "fireball" was. But everyone agreed his nickname should be "Rapid Robert."

Feller's father had taught him how to pitch. Each night he practiced on a field his father built on their Iowa farm. If it was cold or rainy, practice would be in the barn. The hard work paid off. Feller pitched his first major league game when he was just 17—and struck out 15 batters.

BOB FELLER AND HIS DAD

Facing Greenberg and the Tigers, Feller was better than ever. He fanned 18, setting a new strikeout mark. Greenberg whiffed twice, and couldn't break the Babe's home run record. It would stand for another 23 years.

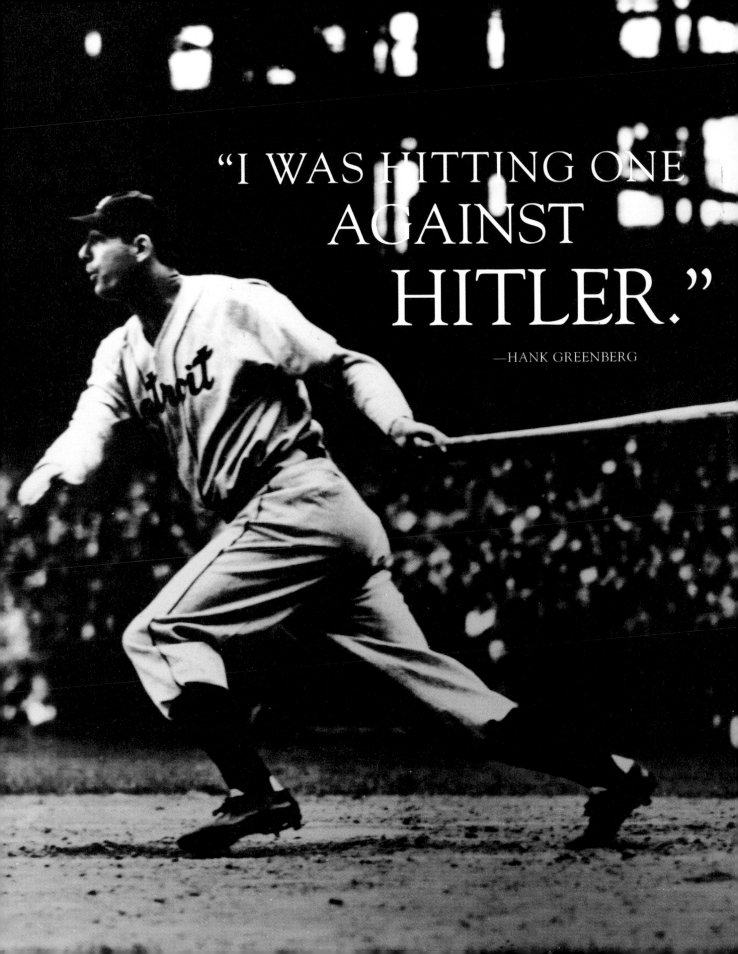

"I WAS HITTING ONE AGAINST HITLER."

—HANK GREENBERG

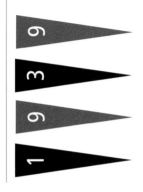

LOU GEHRIG seemed like the healthiest and strongest of baseball players. He'd been nicknamed "the Iron Horse" because nothing kept him off the field. In fact, he hadn't missed a game for almost 14 years.

But in 1939, Gehrig began to play like an old man. He was only 35, yet he could barely run or hit the ball. In the field, he wasn't able to make even the easy plays. He had always been so fit, but now he fell down just changing his clothes.

On May 2, Gehrig took himself out of the lineup. For the first time in 2,130 games, he wasn't at first base for New York. Fans wondered what was wrong with the Yankee cleanup hitter. Doctors found he was suffering from a rare disease called amyotrophic lateral sclerosis, or ALS. It was destroying his nerves and muscles. Gehrig wasn't just sick—he was dying.

On July 4, 1939, Lou Gehrig came to Yankee Stadium for the last time. Sixty-two thousand fans poured in to honor a man who had given them some of their most exciting baseball memories. A Triple Crown winner in 1934, Gehrig had won the Most Valuable Player Award two times. He holds the record for most grand slams (23) and the most RBIs in a single American League season (184).

Throughout his career, Gehrig had always played in Babe Ruth's shadow. The Babe got all the attention, while Lou quietly did a great job. But now the fans wanted him to realize how much they appreciated him. They kept shouting his name until they were hoarse. His number (4) was retired that day, the first time a player was honored in this way.

Weeping, Gehrig took the field to give his thanks. He could barely stand, but said, "Fans, you have been reading about a bad break I got. Yet today I consider myself the luckiest man on the face of the earth."

Gehrig was dead less than two years later. ALS is now commonly known as Lou Gehrig's disease. Gehrig's record of 2,130 consecutive games stands to this day.

LOU GEHRIG

"...THE LUCKIEST MAN ON THE FACE OF THE EARTH."

—LOU GEHRIG

LOU GEHRIG PREPARES TO SAY GOOD-BYE TO THE NEW YORK FAITHFUL AT YANKEE STADIUM. EVEN THOUGH THEY NEVER GOT ALONG, A RETIRED BABE RUTH SHOWED UP TO HUG HIS FORMER TEAMMATE.

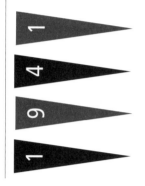

1941. Americans were worried. World War II was raging across three continents—how much longer could the United States stay out of the fighting? Yet that same year, two great players had remarkable seasons. For a little while, they took the nation's mind off the war.

It started routinely enough. On May 15, Joe DiMaggio singled. No one was excited—after all, Joltin' Joe had been the American League batting champ the last two years. He was the Yankees' star center fielder, and made every play look easy. Yet he wasn't as popular as some of his teammates—many fans thought he was cold. But Joe was just shy—he guarded his privacy and never showed his emotions.

After that single, DiMaggio kept on hitting. Twenty, 30, 40 games went by, and Joe had at least one hit in every one of them. It seemed that nothing could stop his streak. When someone stole his favorite bat, he borrowed a teammate's and got another hit—and broke the American League record. Fans who had booed him earlier now applauded his every move.

This wasn't DiMaggio's first long hitting streak. When he was still in the minors, he'd hit in 61 games in a row. But this time, things were different—now he was facing the best pitching in the world. It would be tough to break the major league record of hitting in 44 straight games—a record that had stood for 44 years. But all across the country, people were watching and rooting for Joe.

The streak put DiMaggio under terrible pressure. It was hard to be a hero all the time. He couldn't sleep, and his stomach often bothered him. On the outside he was calm, but as he later said, "That doesn't mean I wasn't dying inside."

On July 2, the Yankee Clipper smacked a home run to break the major league consecutive-game hit record. The only question now was when he would be stopped. By July 17, Joe had hit safely in 56 straight games. That day the Yankees played the Indians in Cleveland. Over 67,000 fans came out to see if Joe could keep hitting. Twice he smashed hard grounders down the third-base line, yet twice the third baseman

JOE POSES AFTER TYING THE MAJOR LEAGUE CONSECUTIVE-GAME HIT RECORD.

turned them into outs. Still, in his last at-bat, it looked as if he'd done it again. He cracked the ball right up the middle—but then it took a bad hop. It bounced toward the shortstop—and DiMaggio was thrown out.

The streak was over, after 56 singles, 16 doubles, four triples, and 15 home runs. But the very next day, Joe went out and began another one. This one lasted 16 games. Altogether, DiMaggio hit safely in 72 out of 73 contests. No player has ever had such a remarkable stretch of games.

With DiMaggio's streak over, attention shifted to the Red Sox's Ted Williams. All season long he'd been hitting well over .400. But toward the end of the season, his average had plunged 13 points—he was now barely above the magic mark. If he could just hit .400 for the season, he'd be among baseball's best.

"I WAS DYING INSIDE."

—JOE DIMAGGIO

The Splendid Splinter had always wanted to be the greatest hitter who ever lived. He was patient even as a child, and taught himself to swing only at strikes. But Williams had a terrible temper, sometimes spitting at fans who booed him. Some believed he was selfish, thinking only about his batting average, not his team.

Williams's battle to hit .400 came down to the final day of the season. The Red Sox were playing a doubleheader against the Philadelphia Athletics. With his average at .3995, Williams could have stayed on the bench—league officials would have rounded it off to .400. The Red Sox manager asked Ted if he wanted to sit the two games out. But Ted told him, "It's not a record unless you play all the way."

Only 23 years old, Williams was feeling the strain. The night before, he'd walked for miles, worrying about the next day's games. But the crowd in the Philadelphia ballpark was behind him completely. Even some of the players on the opposing team wished him luck. At the plate the umpire advised him to relax. Still, he was so nervous his hands were shaking.

But when the pitch came in, he lined it hard for a single. Next time he homered—he had his .400! Yet he wouldn't sit down. He was going to play every inning of both games.

At the end of the day, Ted had six hits. One was such a hard line drive that it dented an outfield loudspeaker. By the time the doubleheader was over, Williams was hitting .406.

He won the batting championship easily that season. But he also led the league in walks (145), homers (37), runs scored (135), slugging percentage (.735), and on-base percentage (.551). While doing all this, he struck out only 27 times.

Baseball has yet to have another year like 1941. No one has hit .400 since Ted Williams. And, in over 50 years, not one major leaguer has come close to breaking Joe DiMaggio's record. For baseball, 1941 was a year to remember.

TED WILLIAMS

"RUN AND HIDE BEHIND SECOND BASE."

—LOU BOUDREAU,
ON WHAT TO DO AFTER YOU
PITCH TO TED WILLIAMS

TED WILLIAMS FELT THAT
HITTING A BASEBALL IS THE
MOST DIFFICULT TASK IN
SPORTS. BUT HE WAS MUCH
BETTER AT IT THAN MOST,
LEADING THE LEAGUE IN
HITTING SIX TIMES.

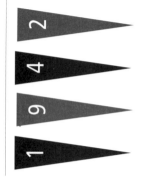

JULY 21, 1942. A battle was on between two great Negro league teams—the Kansas City Monarchs and the Homestead Grays. The man on the mound for the Monarchs was LeRoy Robert "Satchel" Paige, black baseball's greatest pitcher.

It was the ninth inning, and there were two men out. The Monarchs were holding on to a small lead. When a Grays' batter suddenly tripled, Satchel did the unexpected. Instead of trying to get the last out, he walked the next two men on purpose. Now the bases were loaded, and Josh Gibson was due up. Known as the black Babe Ruth, Gibson was the league's outstanding slugger. Satchel was daring him to win the game with one swing.

Years before, Gibson and Paige had been teammates. Each believed he was the greatest player in black baseball. Gibson had once said, "I hit [Satchel] about like every other pitcher."

Satchel hissed back: "See how you can hit my fast one." Now each man had the chance to prove that he was the best. But as Gibson stepped into the batter's box, Satchel called for time. He always knew how to make tight situations even more dramatic. He asked for a glass of water and popped in a pill. The drink foamed and fizzed, and Satchel drank it down. Then he belched and announced, "Now I'm ready."

Forty thousand fans got to their feet. Paige hollered to Gibson, "I'm gonna throw you some fastballs."

Josh didn't move. His bat lay still on his shoulder. Satchel threw.

SATCHEL PAIGE

"Strike one!" the umpire shouted.

Satchel yelled out again: "This is gonna be faster."

Again, Gibson stood still. Strike two!

Now Satchel cried out: "I'm gonna throw a pea at your knee!"

Strike three! Paige strode off the field and had the last word: "*Nobody* hits Satchel."

Written records weren't usually kept in the Negro

"NOBODY HITS SATCHEL."

—SATCHEL PAIGE

leagues, but many believe Satchel won 2,000 games in his career, including 250 shutouts and 45 no-hitters. He reportedly struck out 22 batters in one game.

Gibson didn't let many pitchers get the best of him. Some said this power hitter had arms like sledgehammers. It is believed he batted .457 one year, and in another hit 75 home runs. Many think he clouted 1,000 over his career.

When Satchel Paige faced Josh Gibson, it was one of baseball's most exciting duels. But the two greatest Negro league stars never faced each other in the majors. Paige signed with the Indians in 1948, becoming baseball's oldest rookie. Gibson had already died of a stroke, at the age of 35.

Both Satchel Paige and Josh Gibson are now in the Hall of Fame.

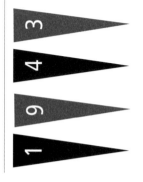

THE YEAR WAS 1943. With hundreds of major leaguers fighting in World War II, baseball teams were stocked with second-rate players. Stadium crowds were shrinking fast.

Then a chewing-gum tycoon named P. K. Wrigley had an idea. He knew fans would come out to watch well-played games. So he started a new league, for women only. It was called the All-American Girls Professional Baseball League. Its athletes were unknown—but they were great ballplayers.

It wasn't the first time women had played professionally. There had been a Young Ladies Baseball Club in Philadelphia in the 1880s. Alta Weiss, "the Girl Wonder," had pitched for a men's team in 1907. In a 1931 exhibition game, 17-year-old Jackie Mitchell had struck out both Babe Ruth and Lou Gehrig!

But women had never had their own league, and hundreds flocked to Chicago for the tryouts. They soon discovered that they were expected to be more than fine athletes. Unlike male players, they had to be good-looking and graceful. The Queens of Swat, as they were known, were supposed to be ladies.

They played in short skirts, which meant they burned their skin every time they slid. Off the field, they had a dress code and were chaperoned to enforce the rules. They were required to go to charm school to learn "proper" manners.

In spite of the strict rules, almost 500 women played for the league's eight teams. They came from all over the United States and Canada. But as in the majors, no blacks were allowed.

The league lasted 12 years, remaining popular long after baseball's male stars returned from the war. Thousands of fans turned out to watch and saw that women could play as well as men. Jean Faut pitched two perfect games, and Joanne Weaver hit .429. Sophie Kurys stole 201 bases in 203 tries and was nicknamed "Tina Cobb."

But today, the majors remain closed to women. Although men of any

JEAN FAUT, STAR PITCHER FOR THE SOUTH BEND BLUE SOX

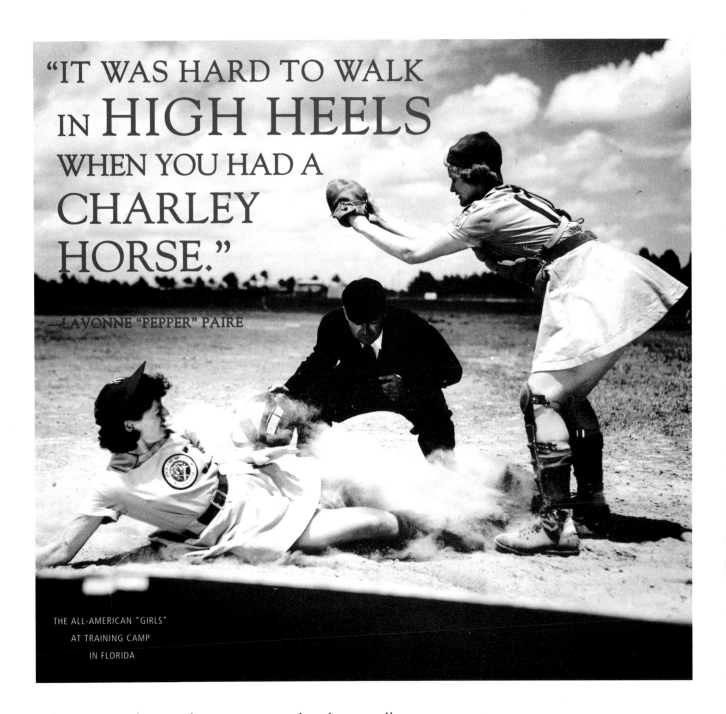

"IT WAS HARD TO WALK IN HIGH HEELS WHEN YOU HAD A CHARLEY HORSE."

—LAVONNE "PEPPER" PAIRE

THE ALL-AMERICAN "GIRLS"
AT TRAINING CAMP
IN FLORIDA

color or strength are welcome, women who play as well as men are not regarded as equal.

Still, women love baseball, and somehow they always find a way to play the game. In 1994, a new all-women's team, the Colorado Silver Bullets, was established to compete in exhibitions against major league farm clubs. At long last, baseball may finally be learning that it can never truly be the sport of all Americans until women are allowed to take the field.

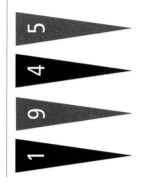

ROBINSON WITH
BRANCH RICKEY

IT WAS 1945, and World War II had ended. Americans of all races had died for their country. Yet black men were still not allowed in the major leagues. The national pastime was loved by all America, but the major leagues were for white men only.

Branch Rickey of the Brooklyn Dodgers thought that was wrong. He was the only team owner who believed blacks and whites should play together. Baseball, he felt, would become even more thrilling, and fans of all colors would swarm to his ballpark.

Rickey decided his team would be the first to integrate. There were plenty of brilliant Negro league players, but he knew the first black major leaguer would need much more than athletic ability.

Many fans and players were prejudiced—they didn't want the races to play together. Rickey knew the first black player would be cursed and booed. Pitchers would throw at him; runners would spike him. Even his own teammates might try to pick a fight.

But somehow this man had to rise above that. No matter what happened, he must never lose his temper. No matter what was said to him, he must never answer back. If he had even one fight, people might say integration wouldn't work.

When Rickey met Jackie Robinson, he thought he'd found the right man. Robinson was 28 years old, and a superb athlete. In his first season in the Negro leagues, he hit .387. But just as importantly, he had great intelligence and sensitivity. Robinson was college-educated, and knew what joining the majors would mean for blacks. The grandson of a slave, he was proud of his race and wanted others to feel the same.

In the past, Robinson had always stood up for his rights. But now Rickey told him he would have to stop. The Dodgers needed "a man that will take abuse."

At first Robinson thought Rickey wanted someone who was afraid to defend himself. But as they talked, he realized that in this case a truly brave man would have to avoid fighting. He thought for a while, then promised Rickey he would not fight back.

"DETERMINATION
WAS WRITTEN
ALL OVER HIM."

—CLYDE SUKEFORTH, DODGER SCOUT

JACKIE ROBINSON TRIES TO
BEAT YOGI BERRA'S TAG.
JACKIE WAS ONE OF THE
MOST FEARED BASE
RUNNERS OF HIS DAY,
LEADING THE LEAGUE IN
STOLEN BASES HIS
ROOKIE YEAR.

Robinson signed with the Dodgers and went to play in the minors in 1946. Rickey was right—fans insulted him, and so did players. But he performed brilliantly and avoided fights. Then, in 1947, he came to the majors.

Many Dodgers were angry. Some signed a petition demanding to be traded. But Robinson and Rickey were determined to make their experiment work.

On April 15—Opening Day—26,623 fans came out to Ebbets Field. More than half of them were black—Robinson was already their hero. Now he was making history just by being on the field.

The afternoon was cold and wet, but no one left the ballpark. The Dodgers beat the Boston Braves, 5–3. Robinson went hitless, but the hometown fans didn't seem to care—they cheered his every move.

Robinson's first season was difficult. Fans threatened to kill him; players tried to hurt him. The St. Louis Cardinals said they would strike if he took the field. And because of laws separating the races in certain states, he often couldn't eat or sleep in the same places as his teammates.

Yet through it all, he kept his promise to Rickey. No matter who insulted him, he never retaliated.

Robinson's dignity paid off. Thousands of fans jammed stadiums to see him play. The Dodgers set attendance records in a number of cities.

Slowly his teammates accepted him, realizing that he was the spark that made them a winning team. No one was more daring on the base paths or better with the glove. At the plate, he had great bat control—he could hit the ball anywhere. That season, he was named baseball's first Rookie of the Year.

Jackie Robinson went on to a glorious career. But he did more than play the game well—his bravery taught Americans a lesson. Branch Rickey opened a door, and Jackie Robinson stepped through it, making sure it could never be closed again. Something wonderful happened to baseball—and America—the day Jackie Robinson joined the Dodgers.

BROOKLYN'S EBBETS FIELD, WHERE JACKIE MADE HIS MAJOR LEAGUE DEBUT

JACKIE SIGNING
AUTOGRAPHS FOR THE
HOMETOWN FANS

THE SHOT HEARD 'ROUND THE WORLD

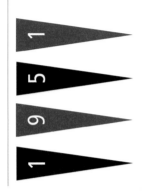

OCTOBER 3, 1951. It was the third and final playoff game to decide the National League pennant. The New York Giants were at home to face their bitter rivals, the Brooklyn Dodgers.

Dodger fans were furious. As late as August, their team had led the Giants by 13½ games. But the Giants went on a winning streak, taking 37 out of their last 44 games. Now the Dodgers were trying to come back. Everything hinged on this last contest.

That afternoon everyone in New York became a fan. As the game got under way, all work seemed to come to a halt. Taxis refused to take passengers, salesmen stopped making sales. People watched TVs in store windows. In the city's jails, prisoners were glued to their radios.

In the bottom of the ninth, the Dodgers led 4–1. It looked as if they would take the pennant after all. But with one out, the Giants scored to make it 4–2. There were two men on base—the next hitter could tie or win the game. To stop the rally, the Dodgers brought in a new pitcher, Ralph Branca. Branca took the mound with only one day's rest.

Into the batter's box stepped Bobby Thomson, the Giants' third baseman. That season he'd hit 32 homers. In the first playoff game, he'd homered off Branca. Now everyone wondered if he could do it again.

Branca threw Thomson a fastball. It nicked the inside corner for strike one. "Should have swung at that," Thomson thought. The next pitch was another fastball, this time high and tight. It was just where Branca wanted it—but Thomson was ready. He slammed the ball toward the left field wall. "Get down!" the Dodger third baseman screamed at the drive. But the ball kept rising—right over the wall! The Giants had taken the game, 5–4. The Dodgers' season was suddenly over.

On the radio, the announcer shouted "The Giants win the pennant!" again and again. Fans on the street yelled so loudly that people high up in office buildings heard them.

Thomson skipped around the bases and was mobbed by his teammates at the plate. Branca left the field and lay down on the clubhouse steps, crying.

BOBBY THOMSON *(ABOVE)* LEFT RALPH BRANCA *(BOTTOM, RIGHT)* CRYING ON THE STEPS OF THE DODGER CLUBHOUSE

To this day, people remember where they were when Thomson hit his homer. The "Shot Heard 'Round the World" was one of baseball's most dramatic endings. Fans learned that no victory is ever certain— after all, the game, as Yogi Berra once said, "ain't over till it's over."

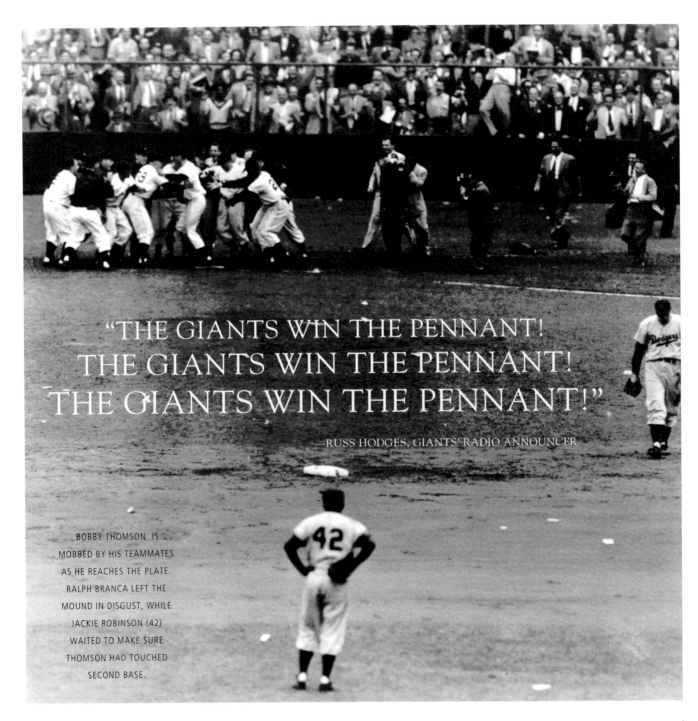

"THE GIANTS WIN THE PENNANT!
THE GIANTS WIN THE PENNANT!
THE GIANTS WIN THE PENNANT!"

—RUSS HODGES, GIANTS' RADIO ANNOUNCER

BOBBY THOMSON IS MOBBED BY HIS TEAMMATES AS HE REACHES THE PLATE. RALPH BRANCA LEFT THE MOUND IN DISGUST, WHILE JACKIE ROBINSON (42) WAITED TO MAKE SURE THOMSON HAD TOUCHED SECOND BASE.

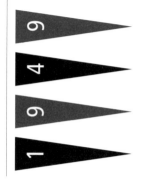

IT ALL BEGAN IN 1949. That was the year nobody thought the Yankees would be a winning club. Their new manager, Casey Stengel, had never won a pennant. Some people thought he was scatterbrained or even stupid because he often jumbled his words, issuing orders like "Everybody line up alphabetically according to your height."

But Stengel knew what he was doing. He deserved his nickname, "the Ol' Perfesser." Nobody in baseball understood the game better.

In 1949, Stengel led the Yankees to victory in the World Series. It was his first championship—but it was only the beginning.

The Yankees stayed on top in 1950 and 1951. After a close call in 1952, when it took them seven games to beat the Dodgers, they won the 1953 Series—their fifth in a row. No other team has ever done that.

During those years, Stengel's Yankees ruled baseball. Some of the game's greatest stars were on his team.

In center field was Mickey Mantle, the best switch hitter ever. Mantle had been injured his rookie year, and played in pain the rest of his career. He was sure he was going to die young, just as his father had, so having fun became the most important thing in his life. He stayed out late, drank too much, and neglected his health. But he was the Yankees' most exciting player, hitting some of baseball's longest home runs. Named Most Valuable Player three times, he won the Triple Crown (the batting, home run, and RBI titles) in 1956.

WHITEY FORD, CASEY'S ACE PITCHER. MICKEY MANTLE DESCRIBED HIM THIS WAY: "COOL. CRAFTY. NERVES OF STEEL."

One of Mantle's best friends was teammate Whitey Ford. The great lefty acted as if he could break any rule. Even with the umpire staring right at him, Whitey would use his ring to scuff the ball. He threw spitballs and mudballs, yet always seemed to get away with it, ending his career with one of the highest winning percentages in this century (.690).

Catcher Yogi Berra seemed so clumsy that one coach called him "the Ape." But Stengel saw his talent, and he became one of baseball's greatest receivers. Yogi won the MVP Award three times.

"I COULDN'T HAVE DONE IT WITHOUT MY PLAYERS."

—CASEY STENGEL, ON WINNING HIS FIFTH WORLD SERIES IN A ROW

CASEY STENGEL *(TOP, CENTER)* CELEBRATES HIS FIRST SERIES VICTORY. YOGI BERRA *(RIGHT)* COMPLETES A DOUBLE PLAY. MICKEY MANTLE *(LEFT)*, ONE OF THE GAME'S STRONGEST *AND* FASTEST PLAYERS, SCORES FOR THE YANKS.

Like Stengel, Yogi was always scrambling his sentences. His sayings are as famous as his old manager's. One of the best-known is, "Baseball is ninety percent physical. The other half is mental."

Casey Stengel was one of the game's most successful skippers. In his 12 years with the Yankees, the team dominated baseball, winning 10 pennants and seven World Series. No other club has been able to match—or even come close to—such a winning tradition.

THE CATCH

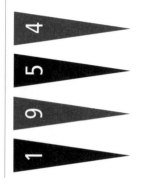

SEPTEMBER 29, 1954. Fifty-three thousand fans were packed into the Polo Grounds to watch the Giants play the Cleveland Indians. It was the top of the eighth in the first game of the World Series. With the score tied 2–2, the Indians had men on first and second with nobody out.

Vic Wertz was up. He already had three hits that day. When the first pitch zipped in, he swung hard and connected. The ball sped toward the Polo Grounds' extra-deep center field. It looked like a triple at least. The Indians seemed set to take the lead.

But out in center field, Willie Mays saw the ball clearly. Without hesitation, he sprinted toward the wall with his back to the plate. He glanced over his left shoulder—he knew he'd have to time this catch perfectly.

Only 10 feet from the wall—450 feet from home plate—Mays was still on the run. He stretched out both arms and opened his glove. The ball dropped in, as though his glove were a magnet. He had outraced the smash.

But the runner on second tagged up. On such a deep fly, he would try to take two bases. Mays had made a perfect catch—now he had to make a perfect throw to second. If he didn't, the Indians would score the tie-breaking run.

In one smooth motion, Mays stopped in his tracks, spun around to face the plate, stepped forward, and flung back his head and arm. When he whipped the ball in, it looked as if he were trying to hurl his whole body. One reporter called it the throw "of a giant."

Mays's cap flew off, and he fell to the ground. "I must have looked like a corkscrew," he said later. But the ball went straight to second base, and the runner had to stop at third. The game remained tied.

When the inning ended, one of Mays's teammates said to him, "I didn't think you were gonna get to that one." Mays calmly replied: "You kiddin'? I had that one all the way."

The Giants went on to win the game and the Series. Mays soon

WILLIE MAYS

became a star. By the time he retired, he ranked third in both home runs (660) and total bases (6,066). Of all outfielders, he recorded the most put-outs (7,752). But not one of them is more famous than his impossible catch in the 1954 Series—the best remembered defensive play in baseball history.

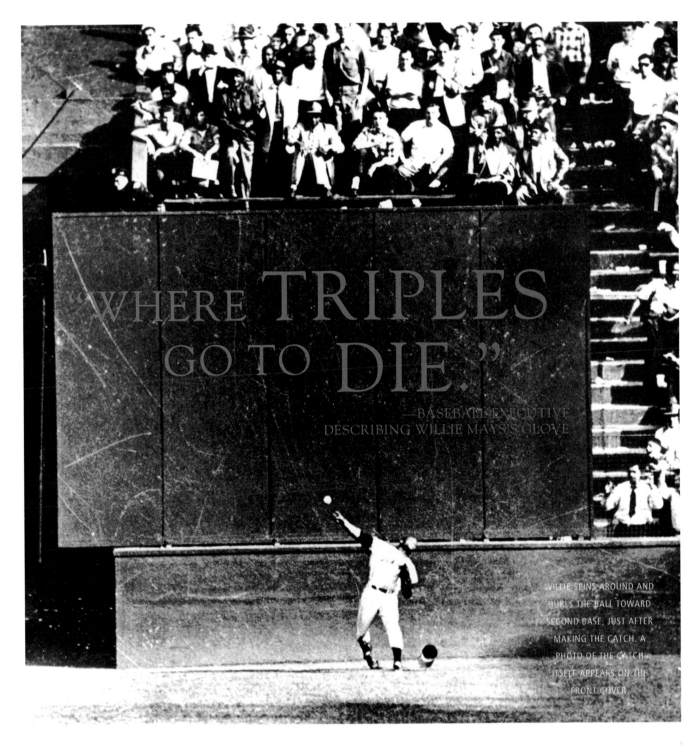

"WHERE TRIPLES GO TO DIE."

—BASEBALL EXECUTIVE
DESCRIBING WILLIE MAYS'S GLOVE

WILLIE SPINS AROUND AND HURLS THE BALL TOWARD SECOND BASE, JUST AFTER MAKING THE CATCH. A PHOTO OF THE CATCH ITSELF APPEARS ON THE FRONT COVER.

PERFECT

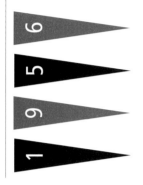

OCTOBER 8, 1956. The Yankees against the Dodgers in the fifth game of the World Series. Not one of the 64,519 fans at Yankee Stadium was expecting to see great Yankee pitching. After all, Don Larsen was on the mound. He'd had a good year, but his arm was unreliable.

But Larsen began this game pitching unusually well. He retired the Dodgers easily in the first. In the second, Jackie Robinson lined a ball that skipped off the third baseman's glove. It bounced right to the short-stop, who threw Jackie out. It seemed Larsen was having a lucky day.

In the fifth, a long fly to left-center looked as if it would drop. But Mickey Mantle dashed over and caught it on the run. Larsen's luck was holding.

In between innings, Don wanted to discuss the game. By now, though, his teammates realized he was pitching a no-hitter. They believed if they talked about it, somehow it wouldn't happen.

It was quiet in the dugout, but Larsen didn't understand why. He said to Mantle, "I'm pitchin' a perfect game here. What do you think about that?" As if some spell might be broken, Mickey didn't reply.

In the eighth inning, a Dodger hit a smash toward the third base-man, but he quickly held up his glove and caught it cleanly.

The crowd grew tense. No one had ever thrown a World Series no-hitter. And Larsen had a shot at something even more exceptional. Not a single Dodger had reached base all afternoon. With no hits, walks, or errors, Larsen was pitching a perfect game.

He got the first two outs in the ninth inning. The next batter came up and took the first pitch for a ball. Don quickly threw two strikes. With the crowd waiting nervously, he threw a pitch that looked a bit high—but the umpire called it strike three. Larsen had his perfect game!

The Yankees beat the Dodgers 2–0 that day, and went on to win the Series. Larsen's feat has never been repeated.

Larsen didn't have a great career—he was 81–91, with a 3.78 ERA. But what fans remember is his one moment of glory. On this day, before an entire nation, Don Larsen was perfect.

DON LARSEN

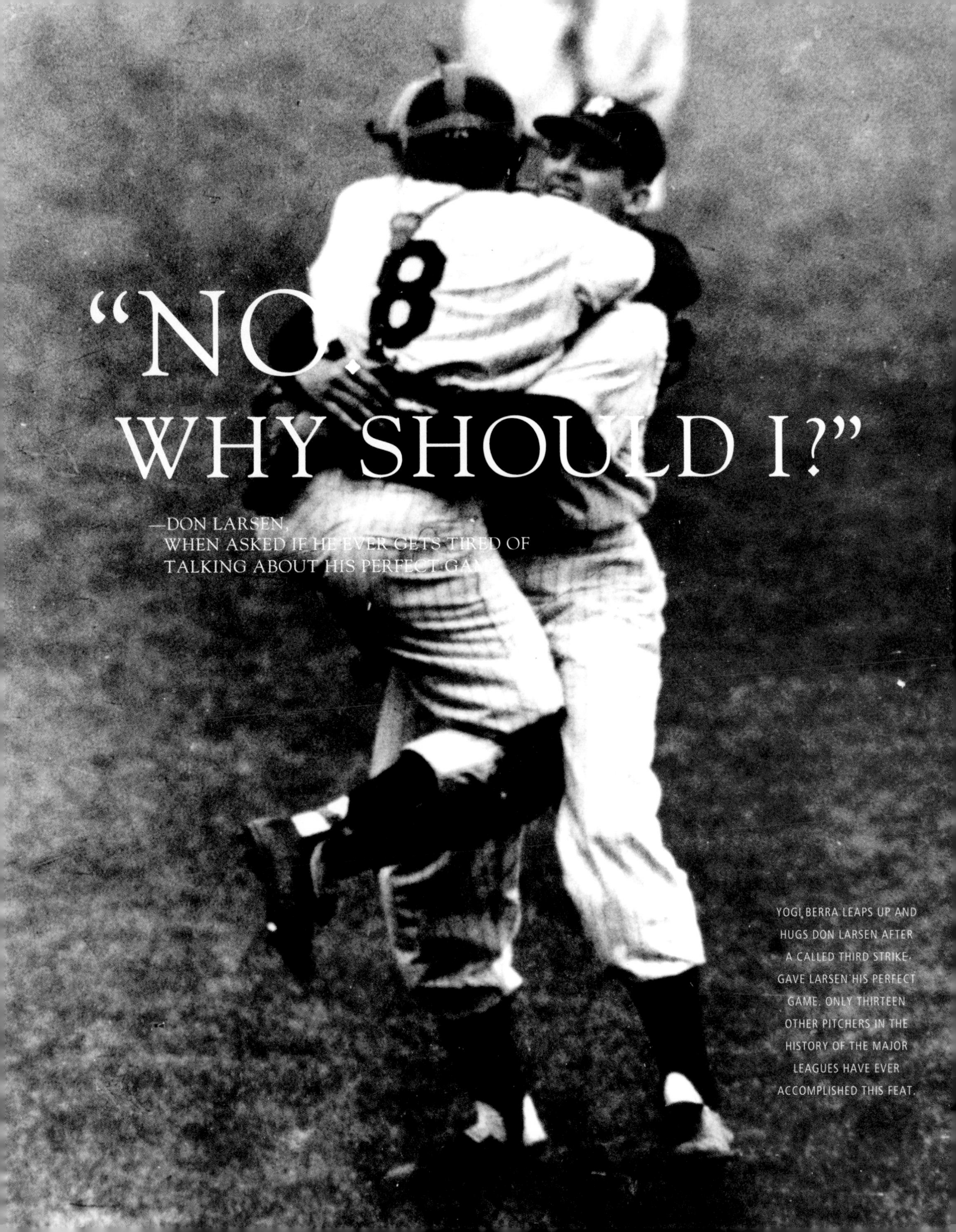

"NO. WHY SHOULD I?"

—DON LARSEN,
WHEN ASKED IF HE EVER GETS TIRED OF
TALKING ABOUT HIS PERFECT GAME

YOGI BERRA LEAPS UP AND
HUGS DON LARSEN AFTER
A CALLED THIRD STRIKE
GAVE LARSEN HIS PERFECT
GAME. ONLY THIRTEEN
OTHER PITCHERS IN THE
HISTORY OF THE MAJOR
LEAGUES HAVE EVER
ACCOMPLISHED THIS FEAT.

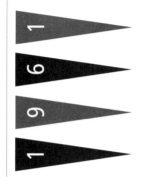

1961

IT WAS 1961. Babe Ruth's record of 60 homers in a season had stood for 34 years. Many believed it would never be broken—certainly not by Roger Maris, the Yankee right fielder. Maris had been named the American League's MVP the year before, but he'd never hit more than 39 homers in a season. He didn't even consider himself a slugger.

But this year was different. He slammed 24 round-trippers in just 38 games. Every time he came to the plate, he swung the bat like a true power hitter. By July 4, he had smashed 31 homers.

Fans began to wonder—could Maris break the Babe's record?

Maris himself never expected it to happen. He said over and over: "I don't want to be Babe Ruth." He was shy and moody, and just wanted to be left alone. Yet the whole world seemed to be watching him.

He didn't like the pressure and became so tense his hair began to fall out. He hated feeling as though he had to hit a homer every time he came to bat. Finally, he asked his manager, "If I can win the game with a bunt, would you mind if I bunted?"

But Maris kept hitting homer after homer. He was chasing the Babe's record whether he wanted to or not.

On September 26, he clouted his 60th home run. Now the record was tied. Could Roger hit another? When the Babe's widow said she hoped he wouldn't, it seemed as though Maris were listening. He sat out one game. Then in the next two, his bat was quiet.

THE STRAIN OF BEING IN THE LIMELIGHT SHOWS ON ROGER MARIS'S FACE.

October 1, the final day of the season, was Maris's last chance to break the record. Fans crowded the right field seats, where he hit most of his blasts. One lucky person might catch the historic ball.

In the fourth inning, Maris came to the plate. Soon the count was two balls and no strikes. The pitcher fired again, whipping in a fastball. But Roger was ready, and hammered it into the right field bleachers.

A few fans fought for the ball while the rest stood and cheered. Maris had done it—he had broken one of baseball's most cherished records. Some were proud of his achievement. Others were angry. They felt that the Babe was the better player and that his record should stand. After all, they said, the Babe had hit 60 homers in 154 games, while Maris's season was longer—162 games.

Maris was just glad the race was over. "All it brought me was headaches," he would later remark. He played only seven more years and never hit as well again. But his record has now stood almost as long as the Babe's.

ROGER CLOUTS HIS 61ST HOME RUN ON THE LAST DAY OF THE 1961 SEASON, BREAKING THE BABE'S RECORD.

"WOULD YOU MIND IF I BUNTED?"

—ROGER MARIS

A HERO RETIRES YOUNG

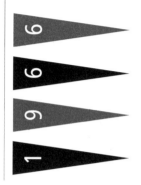

NOVEMBER 18, 1966. Sandy Koufax was about to win his third Cy Young Award, baseball's prize for the best pitcher of the year. It wasn't surprising—from 1963 to 1966, Koufax had the greatest four years of any hurler in history. In 1966, he was 27–9, with a 1.73 ERA. He completed 27 of the 41 games he started, and struck out 317 batters.

Even with a record like Koufax's, winning three awards was quite a feat. Today two pitchers are honored—one from each league—but back then only one could take the prize. Koufax was the first ever to get it three times. Most amazing was the fact that he won with no opposition. In 1963, 1965, and 1966, no other pitcher received a single vote. Sandy is the only man to ever win three Cy Young Awards unanimously.

Yet when Koufax had first started to pitch, he was so wild he sometimes couldn't even hit the batting cage. He struggled for seven years— until a catcher gave him a simple tip. He told Koufax not to throw as hard as he could. If he slowed down just a little, he'd have more control. Sandy began to relax on the mound, and was soon unhittable.

With his blazing fastball and devastating curve, he led the National League in ERA five straight years—a new record. He threw four no-hitters, including a perfect game. He allowed the second fewest hits per game ever and had the second most strikeouts per contest.

But he wasn't just a skilled athlete—he was also a man of principle. He never cheated, or argued with umpires, or lost his temper in a game. And because he was Jewish, Koufax refused to pitch a World Series game that was scheduled to fall on Yom Kippur, the holiest Jewish day.

In 1966, the Dodger left-hander was at the peak of his career. Only 30 years old, Koufax had been playing for just 12 years. It looked as if he would be unbeatable for many seasons to come. Yet today he made an announcement that shocked all of baseball. He had decided to retire.

Something was wrong with his arm, and had been for a while. In order to pitch, he needed special shots to kill the pain. Before every game, he applied heat to his arm, and afterward he had to soak it in ice water.

SANDY KOUFAX
ANNOUNCES HIS
RETIREMENT.

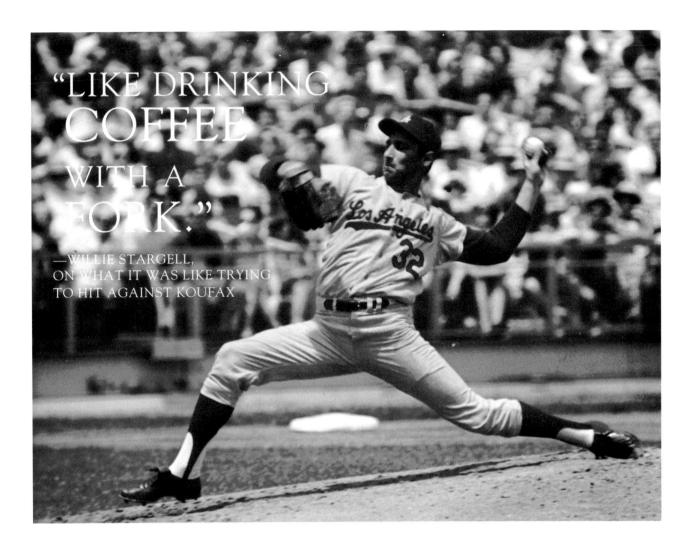

Still, his arm was always swollen. At times he couldn't even raise it high enough to comb his hair.

Despite his injury, he had been pitching brilliantly. Many people didn't know why he would stop. Wasn't the game more important than anything?

Koufax felt his health should come first. It wasn't the pain that bothered him—it was the medication. He didn't want to keep taking painkillers and pills, because no one knew how they would affect him in the future. "I don't regret one minute of the last twelve years," he told reporters, "but I think I would regret one year that was too many." Koufax suspected that if he didn't stop pitching, his arm might be permanently damaged.

Not many athletes can give up the game they love, even when they know it's hurting their bodies. It's hard to step out of the spotlight and turn your back on wealth and fame. But Koufax knew when to stop. In 1972, he became the youngest player ever elected to the Hall of Fame.

AFTER SEEING SANDY PITCH IN 1963, YOGI BERRA SAID, "I CAN SEE HOW HE WON TWENTY-FIVE GAMES. WHAT I DON'T UNDERSTAND IS HOW HE LOST FIVE."

NUMBER 3,000

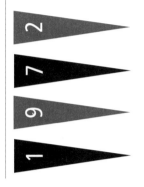

IT WAS SEPTEMBER 30, 1972, the last day of the regular baseball season. Roberto Clemente stepped into the batter's box. His Pirates were playing the New York Mets in Pittsburgh. Though the game wasn't important—the Pirates had already won their division—thousands were at the ballpark. They knew Clemente was swinging for his 3,000th hit.

In 1972, only nine other players had ever accomplished this feat. Just the day before, Clemente thought he'd finally done it. He'd hit a slow ground ball he knew he could beat out. But when the second baseman bobbled it, it was ruled an error. Clemente was angry—he thought he'd been robbed.

It wasn't the first time Clemente thought he had been treated unfairly. He was a great player, but was often harassed because he was Puerto Rican and black. He frequently played while hurt, but was nonetheless accused of imagining his injuries. The Pirates called him Bobby, not Roberto, to make him seem more American. But he was proud of his heritage and insisted on Roberto.

Despite it all, he had a brilliant career. He was an All-Star 12 times, hit over .300 for 13 seasons, and was one of the greatest outfielders in baseball history. One teammate said that when Clemente was out in right field, "it was like having four outfielders."

Now, with Roberto at the plate, every fan stood and cheered. They wanted him to get a hit almost as much as he did. The first pitch was a strike. But the next was a curveball that he whacked to left for a double. It was his 3,000th hit—Clemente had realized his dream.

ROBERTO CLEMENTE

Tragically, he never played another season. In December of that year, an earthquake destroyed much of Nicaragua. Months after Clemente led the Pirates to a division title, he volunteered to help fly supplies to people in need. Just after takeoff, his plane burst into flames and crashed into the sea. His body was never found. He was just 38 years old.

As much a hero to his people as Jackie Robinson was to African Americans, Roberto Clemente was the first Latino in the Hall of Fame.

While there are now 17 players with 3,000 or more hits, Clemente's achievement is still extraordinary. No one watching that day suspected his 3,000th would be his last.

"HE GIVES HIS LIFE FOR SOMEBODY HE DON'T KNOW."

—TEAMMATE MANNY SANGUILLEN

ROBERTO'S OUTSTANDING ABILITIES HELPED PAVE THE WAY FOR HUNDREDS OF LATIN AMERICAN MAJOR LEAGUE BALLPLAYERS.

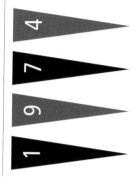

APRIL 8, 1974. That night, the Braves were playing the Los Angeles Dodgers. More than 50,000 fans had jammed into Atlanta Stadium to see if Hank Aaron could make history. Just a few days before, he had tied Babe Ruth's career home run record of 714. Now he could break it.

All across America, people were watching the game on TV. Most were rooting for Aaron, but some didn't want him to succeed. The Babe was still baseball's most admired player, and many people didn't want a black man to outdo him. There was such prejudice against Aaron that he had received death threats. The FBI was called in, and bodyguards escorted him everywhere he went.

The intolerance of others was not new to Hank. He was born poor in Alabama, and began his career in the Negro leagues. Though he came to the majors seven years after Jackie Robinson, his experience was similar to Robinson's. Fans and players cursed him, pitchers threw at his head. In the South, he was not allowed to stay in white team-mates' hotels or eat in the same restaurants.

All this only made Aaron more determined. He was a quiet, proud man who never showed off. Other players got more attention, but Aaron got more hits. Over his 23-year career, he was baseball's most consistent slugger.

It was the fourth inning, and just past nine at night. The count on Aaron was 1-and-0 when the pitcher made a mistake and threw a slider right down the middle. Hank lined it to left-center. Everyone in the stadium heard the crack of the bat.

Aaron didn't think his smash had enough height. But the ball rose and sped over the wall. The crowd stood and roared as fireworks boomed and sparkled above. Aaron had hit number 715—the record was all his.

As he circled the bases, Hank felt as if he were in a daze. Everything seemed to be moving in slow motion. Two college students

HANK AARON

leapt from the stands and patted his back as he rounded second. At home plate all his teammates tried to lift him on their shoulders. Weeping, he turned to his parents, who had come out onto the field. "I never knew," he said later, "that my mother could hug so tight."

A writer once said that Aaron, nicknamed "Hammer," was "the man who did the most with a baseball bat." He is one of only four players to get 3,000 hits, 300 home runs, and 200 stolen bases. He holds the major league records for most lifetime home runs (755), RBIs (2,297), total bases (6,856), and extra-base hits (1,477).

Possibly because Aaron had never hit 50 home runs in a season, it wasn't until the end of his career that people realized what a great player he was. But this record-breaking blast finally put him where he belonged—on top. Number 715 made him the new home run king.

HANK LET HIS BAT DO THE TALKING. HERE HE ROUNDS THE BASES AFTER BELTING NUMBER 715, BREAKING THE BABE'S HOME RUN RECORD.

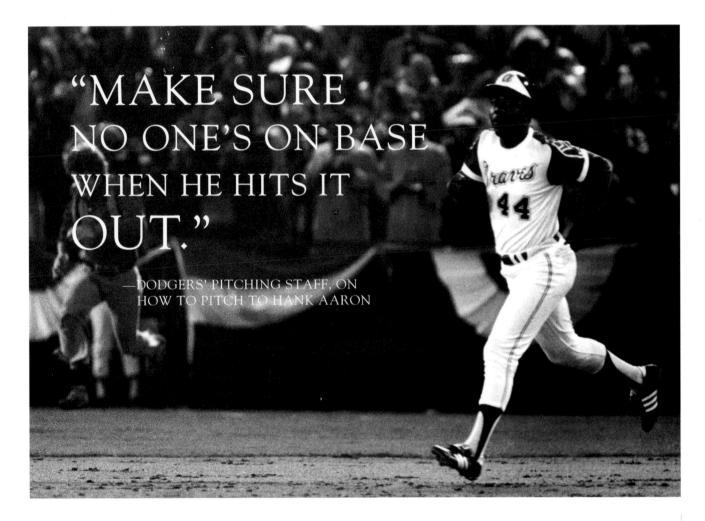

"MAKE SURE NO ONE'S ON BASE WHEN HE HITS IT OUT."

—DODGERS' PITCHING STAFF, ON HOW TO PITCH TO HANK AARON

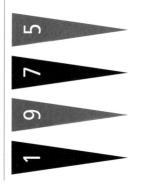

1975

OCTOBER 21, 1975. It was the sixth game of the World Series between the Boston Red Sox and the Cincinnati Reds. Rain had kept the teams out of Boston's Fenway Park for three days. With the Reds leading the Series three games to two, the Sox knew they had to win. But the score was tied 6–6 in the bottom of the 12th—it was anybody's ball game.

Millions of people were watching on TV. Just when it seemed that the country was bored with baseball, this World Series had rekindled national interest. So far it had been one of the best ever, full of close contests and come-from-behind victories. Now fans were being treated to one of the most exciting baseball games ever. Trailing 6–3 in the eighth inning, the Sox had rallied to send the game into extra innings.

Now the Red Sox were batting in the bottom of the inning. Their catcher, Carlton "Pudge" Fisk, was leading off. He had been injured most of the year and was now determined to help his team. Every fan was thinking the same thing—would Fisk get a pitch he could drive?

CARLTON FISK HITS ONE HIGH AND DEEP *(BELOW)*, THEN URGES IT FAIR *(RIGHT)*. HIS BLAST ENDED ONE OF THE MOST EXCITING POST-SEASON GAMES EVER PLAYED.

With the count 1-and-0, the pitcher delivered low. But Fisk was a low-ball hitter. He swung hard and smacked the pitch deep to left field. It looked far enough and high enough to clear the tall left field wall called the Green Monster—but would it stay fair? It seemed as if it might hook foul into the stands.

Fisk started toward first, then suddenly stopped. He couldn't take his eyes off his drive. As if he could command it with his body, he leaned to the right and waved his arms. His mouth was open—it looked as if he were talking to the ball.

Its flight seemed endless. Everyone in the ballpark stood up and leaned in the same direction as Fisk. At last the ball hit the foul pole—fair ball! It was a home run by the slimmest of margins. The Red Sox had won the game!

Fisk leapt into the air, and fans rushed the field as he rounded the bases. When he reached home plate, he jumped on it with both feet.

Church bells began to ring out all over New England. It was after midnight, but not a fan was asleep. Suddenly baseball seemed like the world's most exciting sport again.

Most fans think this was the most thrilling Series game ever. The two teams never gave up, despite close calls and a lead that kept changing hands. Ultimately the Reds took the championship, scoring the winning run in the ninth inning of the seventh game. But the most vivid image from the Series will always be Carlton Fisk "leaning" the ball fair.

"GO FAIR!"

—BOSTON FANS

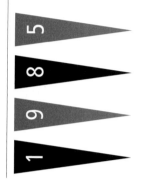

1985

SEPTEMBER 11, 1985. Cincinnati's Riverfront Stadium was packed as the Reds faced the San Diego Padres. Thousands of fans had turned out to root for Pete Rose. Tonight he was trying to break one of baseball's greatest records. His next hit would be his 4,192nd, which would put him past Ty Cobb's 4,191 and make him the man with the most hits ever.

Rose, the Reds' player-manager, was one of America's favorite athletes. But he was 44 years old and had lost many of his baseball skills. Usually a team player, his sights were now set on Cobb's record.

When he first joined the Reds, Rose was a lot like Cobb. Both men wanted to win at any cost. With his headfirst flying slides into any base, he stretched singles into doubles and doubles into triples. Nicknamed "Charlie Hustle" because he ran to first even when he was walked, Rose never gave up and never relaxed. He loved baseball more than anything.

Now Rose wanted to add Cobb's record to his many accomplishments. In the very first inning, with the count 2-and-1, he lifted a pitch into left-center. The ball dropped for a single—and the record was his.

The crowd jumped to its feet and the celebration began. Fireworks exploded, coloring the sky. A Goodyear blimp flashed "Pete Rose, 4,192" high above the stadium. Pete stood on first base and cried. He had waited so long for this moment.

PETE ROSE

When he retired in 1986, Pete Rose had a total of 4,256 hits. He also had the most at-bats (14,053) and appeared in the most games ever (3,562). No one seemed more certain to make the Hall of Fame.

But in 1989, while Rose was still managing the Reds, his gambling addiction was revealed. One of baseball's strictest rules forbids anyone in the sport to bet on ball games. The commissioner believed Rose had ignored the rule, so he was banned from baseball, and the Hall closed its doors to him.

Pete Rose had been a hero for many years. Setting a new hitting mark was a great accomplishment. No one can take his record away from him—but not even a superstar is above the rules.

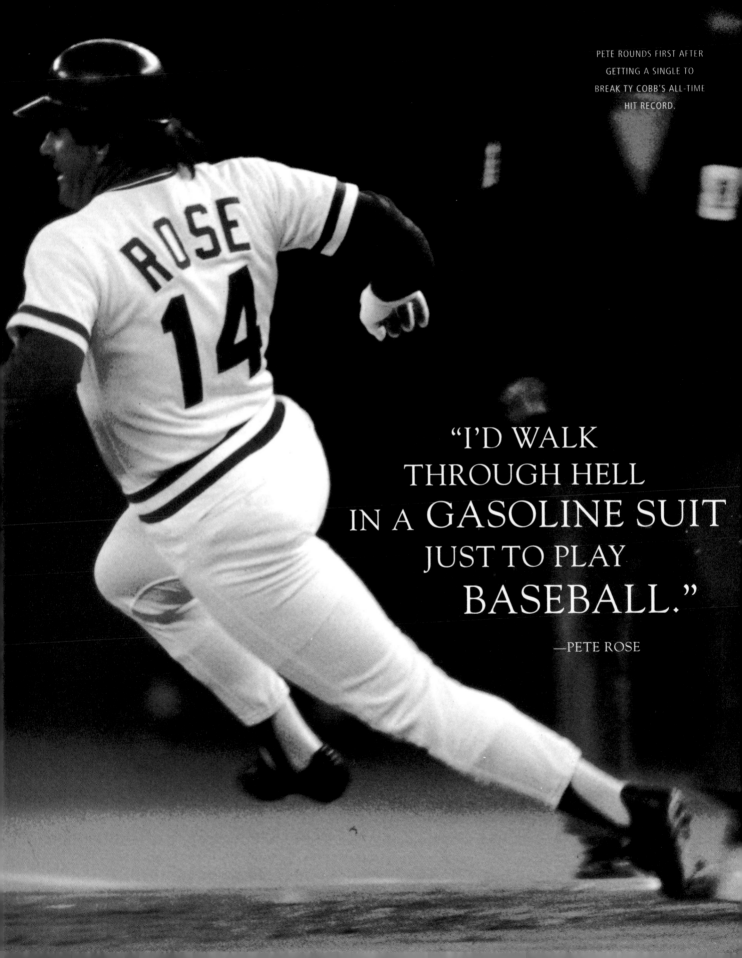

"I'D WALK
THROUGH HELL
IN A GASOLINE SUIT
JUST TO PLAY
BASEBALL."

—PETE ROSE

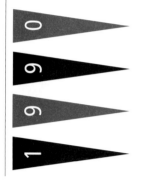

1990
1991

SEPTEMBER 14, 1990. The Seattle Mariners were playing the California Angels. It was the top of the first when 40-year-old Ken Griffey Sr. came to bat. Watching from the on-deck circle was his son, Ken Griffey Jr. The younger Griffey was just 20, but he was already a star.

A year earlier, Ken Sr. had been playing for the Reds, and Ken Jr. was a Mariner rookie. It was the first time a father and son had ever played in the same major league season. They were proud of each other—baseball was a family tradition. Someday, they dreamed, they might play the outfield together. Then, in August, Ken Sr. joined the Mariners, and the dream came true.

Now the Griffeys were the first father and son to be on the same major league team. Ken Sr. waited for the pitch. There was a man on first with no one out. Down two strikes, Ken saw the change-up coming. He lined the ball hard, 402 feet to center. Home run!

Ken Jr. stepped into the batter's box. The pitcher threw him three straight balls. But he smacked the fourth pitch 388 feet to left-center. Home run!

The Griffeys had achieved yet another first—back-to-back homers by father and son. The California crowd had unexpectedly seen baseball history. "What a moment," the Seattle manager said later. "You're never going to see this happen again."

Ken Sr. retired in 1991. In 1992, Ken Jr. was named the All-Star Game's Most Valuable Player. His dad had won the same award 12 years earlier. They're the only father and son in baseball history to accomplish that feat.

By 1993, Ken Jr. was a superstar slugger. Ken Sr. watched him proudly from the stands. As in many baseball-loving families, a father had taught his son to love—and play—the game.

KEN GRIFFEY JR. CONGRATULATES HIS DAD, KEN GRIFFEY SR., FOR HITTING A HOME RUN.

"YOU'LL NEVER SEE THIS HAPPEN AGAIN."

—JIM LEFEBVRE, MARINERS' MANAGER

THE EXPRESS GETS NUMBER SEVEN

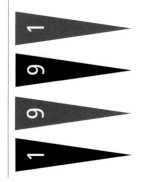

1991

MAY 1, 1991. Arlington Stadium, Texas. Forty-four-year-old Nolan Ryan took the mound for the Rangers. Most players his age would have retired years before, but Ryan just seemed to get stronger every season. This was his 711th game, and he was facing the Toronto Blue Jays. In 1966, when Nolan was a rookie, only three of the Jays had even been born!

Nicknamed "the Express," Nolan had already proved he was a great pitcher. He held 19 strikeout records, and his fastball, clocked at 100.9 miles per hour, was the speediest ever.

Before the game, though, he didn't act like the strikeout king. "I feel old today," he said. "My back hurts, my finger hurts, my ankle hurts, everything hurts." Yet once he began to pitch, he kept getting batters out. His curve was snapping, and his fastball was hitting 96 on the radar gun. The Jays couldn't get their bats on the ball.

Tonight's game was on national TV. Soon fans all over America heard Ryan had a no-hitter going. He had recorded six already—two more than any other pitcher. Nobody at the game that night—especially Nolan—thought he'd be going for his seventh. If he succeeded, he'd be the oldest man to allow no hits in a game.

History was being made, and everyone knew it. In Texas, there was a traffic jam as people rushed to the stadium. With every inning, the crowd got larger. In other ballparks, scoreboards televised the game. When teams finished playing, they rushed to the locker room to watch Nolan on TV.

In the sixth inning, it looked as if Nolan's bid was over. A short fly to center seemed almost certain to drop in for a bloop single. But the outfielder judged it perfectly and made a fine catch. Nolan's no-hitter was still alive.

By the ninth, there were over 33,000 fans in the stands. With two down, Roberto Alomar, one of the Jays' best batters, came up. But Ryan, with all his experience, stayed calm. He struck out Alomar easily. Incredible as it seemed, he had pitched his seventh no-hitter.

NOLAN RYAN

The crowd cheered, and Nolan's teammates lifted him onto their shoulders.

Ryan had won the game, 3–0. He had walked two batters and struck out 16. Only four Jays had managed to hit balls to the outfield. Later, Nolan called it his "most overpowering night."

Modest as ever, Ryan didn't go out and celebrate. Just as he did after every game, he rode his exercise bike for 45 minutes.

When he retired in 1993, Nolan Ryan had the most strikeouts ever (5,668) and the most strikeouts in a single season (383). But his most exciting game was the one everyone thought was impossible—pitching a seventh no-hitter at the age of 44.

NOLAN RYAN'S TEAMMATES HELP HIM CELEBRATE AFTER HE PITCHED HIS SEVENTH NO-HITTER.

"I FEEL OLD TODAY."

—NOLAN RYAN

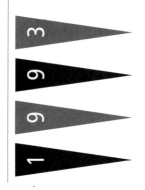

OCTOBER 24, 1993, 11:39 P.M. Toronto's SkyDome was packed with over 50,000 people. It was the bottom of the ninth in the sixth game of the World Series. The Blue Jays led the Series three games to two, but the Philadelphia Phillies were leading this game, 6–5.

Mitch Williams, nicknamed "Wild Thing," was the Phillies' pitcher. He walked Rickey Henderson on four straight balls. Devon White then flied out, but Paul Molitor singled. Now the Jays' clean-up hitter, Joe Carter, was up.

The Phillies were tense. They had the lead, but Williams was unpredictable. He might strike the batter out—or he might not be able to find the plate. One of his teammates couldn't bear to watch. He sat on the bench with a towel over his head.

Joe Carter waited for the pitch. He had always dreamed about this moment. As a little boy, he had imagined hitting a game-winning home run. Now, if he could slug the ball over the fence, he would become one of baseball's great heroes.

After three pitches, the count was 2-and-1. Williams delivered a slider, and Carter swung and missed. Darren Daulton, the Phillies' catcher, signaled for another slider. But with the count 2-and-2, Williams threw a fastball. He aimed for the outside corner, but got the ball down and in. Carter swung smoothly and smashed it 379 feet.

Everyone watched the long fly ball—except Joe. He lost it in the lights. But as he neared first, he saw it speed over the left field wall. His dream had come true. He'd won the game—and the World Series— with a homer!

The crowd went wild. Fireworks went off, filling the SkyDome. Carter leapt around the bases, jumping up and down like a little boy. When he reached home plate, his teammates surrounded him. He couldn't help feeling he was now part of history. "Yes," he said later, "I do believe in miracles."

Williams left the field and went silently to his locker. All he could

JOE CARTER

do was sit and stare at the floor. He told reporters he felt terrible for letting his teammates down.

The Blue Jays had now won two championships in a row. They were the first team since the 1978 Yankees to win back-to-back Series.

Joe Carter is the only player ever to hit a come-from-behind homer to win a World Series. As he went to meet the press, he was stopped by a little boy. "You're the best, Joe," the child told him. That night, millions of baseball fans agreed.

"I DO BELIEVE IN MIRACLES."
—JOE CARTER

JOE'S TEAMMATES SURROUND HIM AT HOME PLATE. JOE'S THREE-RUN HOMER INSTANTLY ENDED THE PHILLIES' DREAM OF A WORLD SERIES VICTORY.

INDEX

Photo credits:
Allsport USA: A. D. Steele/Allsport USA, 54; AP/Wide World Photos: 39 (top), 39 (right), 50, 51, 53, 56–60; Associated Press: 41, 46; Bettmann Archive: 19 (bottom), 23, 38, 39 (left); Brooklyn Public Library: 34; Brown Brothers: 9; Camera 5/Ken Regan: 47, 48; Cleveland Public Library: 35; DOT/Carl Skalak: 55; Florida State Archives: 31; George Eastman House/Nickolas Muray: 18; William Gladstone: 32; Dennis Goldstein: 14, 29; Family of Walter Johnson/Henry Thomas: 15; Kirk M. Kandle: 19 (top); Library of Congress: 43; Los Angeles Dodgers, Inc./Barney Stein: 36; National Baseball Library & Archive, Cooperstown, N.Y.: 7 (bottom), 8, 12, 13, 16, 17, 20, 24–26, 28, 37, 40, 42, 44; National Baseball Library & Archive, Cooperstown, N.Y./Nat Fein: 5; Marvin Newman: 49; Northern Indiana Historical Society: 30; Carl Seid: 21; Corey R. Shanus: 6, 7 (top), 10; The Sporting News: 11, 22; Sports Illustrated/Walter Iooss, 1; Sports Illustrated/Mark Kauffman, 33; Sports Illustrated/Chuck Solomon, 61; Sports Illustrated/Tony Triolo: 52; Robert Stanley: 27; UPI/Bettmann: 45.

THIS IS A BORZOI BOOK PUBLISHED BY ALFRED A. KNOPF, INC.

Library of Congress Cataloging-in-Publication Data

Ward, Geoffrey C.
25 great moments / by Geoffrey C. Ward and Ken Burns, with S. A. Kramer.
p. cm. — (Baseball, the American epic)
Includes index.
ISBN 0-679-86751-1 (trade) — ISBN 0-679-96751-6 (lib. bdg.)
1. Baseball—United States—History—Juvenile literature.
[1. Baseball—History.] I. Burns, Ken. II. Kramer, Sydelle. III. Title.
IV. Title: Twenty-five great moments. V. Series.
GV863.A1B85 1994
796.357'0973—dc20 94-1674

Manufactured in the United States of America
2 4 6 8 0 9 7 5 3 1